a collection of poetry

vol. one

Joe Cundiff

Published by NeMours Publishers, LLC
Copyright © 2019 Joe Cundiff

Editors: Timothy Sams, Jenny Yonkman Bangma
Cover Photography & Design: Joe Cundiff
Author Pages: https://joecundiff.com/
https://YouTube.com/c/joecundiff
@joecundiffauthor

ISBN:9781698539447

DEDICATION

This book is dedicated to all the friends and family that never told me I was crazy to pursue this dream, my writing journey. It takes a lot sometimes to put yourself out there, not knowing how your words might be received, because they're more than words. Writing, especially poetry, comes from a much deeper place. Without your love and support, I would have never found the courage to make this happen. Bringing this poetry journey to life, has been one of my greatest joys. I simply can't express how much it means. Thank you for believing.

CONTENTS

ACKNOWLEDGMENTS

Once again, I would like to think my editors - Jenny Yonkman Bangma and Timothy Sams.   I lean on you two a lot, and you always come through. Your advice and input, on writing and life, is always solid and what I need to hear. Even when I don't want to hear it. Thank you!

As always, there are too many friends and family to thank, which is why this book is dedicated to you. Still, there are a few I must mention.

First, to my brother Mark Cundiff, a big thank you. Though poetry and much of my writing would not make your normal reading list, you always read it anyway, and offer support and encouragement - both with my writing and life. Appreciate you!

And to my cousin, friend, and confidant Karen Tyson, thank you for always being a sounding board of reason. Your support and encouragement means a lot!

To my daughters, Jayde and Jordyn, thank you for always believing in your dad. Love you both! More...

BONUS COVERAGE!

IF YOU ENJOY ANY, OR ALL OF THESE POEMS, PLEASE TUNE IN TO MY YOUTUBE CHANNEL (LINK BELOW) FOR MORE BONUS MATERIAL.

https://YouTube.com/c/joecundiff

I WILL BE MAKING A VIDEO FOR EACH SELECTION, TO SHARE AND DISCUSS WITH YOU THE INSPIRATION AND STORIES BEHIND EACH POEM. I'LL ALSO READ EACH POEM ALOUD.

SO, VISIT MY YouTube CHANNEL, SUBSCRIBE, AND STAY TUNED. I'LL SEND YOU AN EMAIL WITH THE LINK TO EACH NEW EDITION.

BE SURE AND COMMENT YOUR THOUGHTS. I WOULD LOVE TO HEAR FROM YOU!

Dear Reader,

Attempting to measure the meaning of this book with words, is simply not possible. The following pages will unpack over thirty years of my writing journey, with a collection of twenty-nine of my favorite poems. Some I've shared publicly before, but many selections have never seen print. A few I've never shared in any form.

The first poem of this collection is appropriately the first poem I ever wrote. I didn't plan to become a poet. It was not even something I thought about. But this need to try and capture, with words, the way a place feels, burned inside of me. When I could no longer contain the fire, the words spilled out onto the page.

"Places" was my first attempt to capture that feeling with words, and the obsession never left. It has only grown with time, burning deeper into my being with the pass of each new season.

There are a lot of rules to writing, and poetry, and I break all of them. Poetry is art. Art is an expression - an express invitation to the artist's soul. Those brave enough to venture onto the canvas have earned the right to break the rules.

Simply, is my invitation to you. Enjoy!

"The first rule of poetry - is there are no rules with poetry.
Write what you feel, and they will feel what you write."
~simply joe

PLACES

there are places
where time stands still
or so it seems
where life is more than living
living more than feeling
and the feeling
somehow becomes real

these places abound
for all
yet seldom few
ever look
for those who look
they often find
yet what they discover
no volume could bind
for too few are the pages
to capture in a book

the view from here
impossible to define
for it's not what the eye can see
rather what they can feel
no pair feels the same
yet each are linked
as the feeling becomes
real

the view from here
undefined
yet, there's something captive
here
only time could erase
even blind
one could see
the view from here
for it's the smell
the feel
and the air
that draws us near

there's a feeling here
a certain feeling to a place

THE FALLING RAIN

The pitter, the patter
the constant clatter
the drone
of the drowning rain

The birds, their banter
now silent and somber still
safe and serene
subdued
by the canter
of continuous rain

My coat uncloaked
now hooked
and hung on high
the drip
of endless drops
the dripping of the rain

The pitter, the patter
the constant splatter
of pools
and puddles of rain
pooling upon my floor

Never less to mind
what's ever is mine
is never washed
ashore
my love, the rain
is evermore

Undaunted and duly dry
my ear pressed
anxious and aware
and wanton more
what's more, my love
than my love
of the falling rain

simply

EACH DAY DIVINE

how then shall I
define the day
lest the day
shall define me
I must go first
I must decide
if I were to allow
the day its way
its way with me
it will
but rather I
will have my way
with this day
I will have it
my way
I shall decide
and thus define
the day
my day defined
by me
each day then
divine

simply

EMBERS GLOW

there are nights
that I know
the fire
and she
my only friend
her warmth holds more
than merely touch
rather more
my soul
and nights that linger
alone
are never so
yet rather joined
the chorus and chords
of time
and the memories
flow
of one and those
once gathered here
as the embers
glow
slowly fades
my only friend
and memories still
remain

GATES TO NOWHERE

be aware
and wary wise
of the open gates
to nowhere
the path appears
and would appear
to be clear
yet, whence and where
the open field leads
greener grains
of grass
golden weaves
of sunbaked strands
waves beneath the willow's
windswept wave

and the wonders
that await
as one wanders
unaware
from the mist
of morning's rise
each hour slips
sullen away
and subdued
another night's slumber
and beyond
the island of hope

a field of dreams
and a mere glimmer
of light

hard pressed we fall
impressed
into impressionable traps
lured by the allure
of such illustrious
expectations
lurid language
lingers within
and parched our souls
and beckons us
once more
further from
and farther away
from our depths
of desire

so simply we sway
and swayed
into the wake
of decay
betrayed
our hearts only
passion
be aware and wary wise
of the open gates
to nowhere

ON LIMBS OF TREES

it is on a night

and nights like these

when the snow

falls free

and lays heavily and

gracefully in sounds of beauty

on limbs of trees

and it seems

neither an end

nor again will spring

yet the winds no longer

howl

but a bitter chill

persists

and amidst it all

the birds I ponder

and wonder how

warm might they be

and ponder still

nestled on limbs

of trees

how something small

and so seemingly frail

Could be hearty more

than we

SIMPLY

WHISPERING PINES

somewhere

deep within the shadows

of whispering pines

there lurks a spirit of mystery

known only to the natives

and to those brave enough

to seek her out

the slow dance

of days befalling nights

the gentle grind

that moves years

into the weave of a lifetime

only to linger

in the waning hours

of what remains

and the storehouse of memories

beyond the echo of lone howls

therein lies the truth

OF PRIDE AND PASSION

There are the games we play
and there is passion
It is perhaps America's pastime
that merely passes the time
until the tumble of Autumn leaves
ushers in the rumble of the band
the roar of the crowd
and that first whistle blast
It is more than mere game
It is the beating
of our collective hearts
the blood pouring through veins
and spilling on sacred soil
and the breath of life
that conjoins and divides
families friends and foes
into one shimmering cathedral

The stadium lights and Friday night
sights sounds and smells
a confluence of pure harmony
sweetly singing the melodies of our time
drifting past cities and towns
factories and farms
flowing downstream in a single chord
of harmonious rhythm
It is pure
It is passion
It is football

Hidden deep within the confines
of locker rooms and huddles
and the sweat pouring
from pounding iron and colliding pads
there lies an intricately woven bond
that bands boys into men
and brothers forever
Traditions passed down
from one generation to the next
not merely handed out
but emblems and stripes
earned in the gruesome trenches
of a controlled and contrived violence
that is not for all

It was neither manufactured
nor planned
this passion lain meticulously
across our land
As with art
it was bought and paid
with sweat and with tears
and evolved from the raw essence
and purity of pride
A game no less
of cowhide and lace
and fearless warriors
facing off in a grueling grind
to claim their own
that sacred space

Not of hoisting shiny trophies
nor medals nor any grand accolades
these battles are fought and won
and lost
in the trenches of time
that neither time
nor dimming lights may erase
It is rather the mettle to move on
and to rise
to rise above the dust
and mud smeared
across the face
of one's fiercest foe
and when at last
the echo of that final whistle
has blown
to offer a hand of embrace
and to know this was no race

It is pure
It is passion
It is football

SIMPLY

HUCKLEBERRY DREAMS

When, as only a boy
I was
a kid of eight or maybe even ten
Uncertain though I may be
of my age that may have been
it was then, I'm certain
this dream was set to begin
my Huckleberry Dream

A raft set sail
set free
somewhere upstream
abandoned and unmanned
it was set to pass
between the banks and shores
and between the bridges
along the river
that bore all my dreams

There was neither time
to ask
nor reason to wonder
for whence and why it came
For the narrow river
swift as it may
would soon carry my craft
onward, away

Yes, in that moment
I laid claim
the wayward vessel
was now my own
But first therein lay the task
to capture and to sail
a raft with no mast

So I dashed with purpose
and passion
born in a moment
n'er a moment to let pass
without thought or fear
I ran
to reach the shore
and by great fortune
along the way
lay a great long stick
scooped up in stride
a navigator's guide
it soon would be
and further, I ran
pole in hand
along her side
as the river's
flow
when suddenly I soared
from the high bank's perch
I leapt, pole in hand
and it was as if it all
had been planned

and upright
I did land
and aboard my craft
my navigator's hand
sunk one end of my shaft
and discovered the water's sway
yield to my command
to and fray
standing tall atop the wavering raft
suddenly I was free
and proud
as the vessel
and waters
beneath my feet
unleashed unto my world
my Huckleberry Dreams

As it was in that moment
and moments still
to pass
these dreams did dance
and forever would last
and that day began
what each night
would end
as I lay awake in bed

Shadows in the darkness
outside my window
were the endless chirp
of tree frogs chirping
and the echo
of the river's pass
A sweet serenade
that carried my soul
beyond the narrow banks
of my mind
unto an unknown world
mysterious and magically
uncertain
Adrift, soon I fell
to sleep
only to awake
in the wake
of years passed
A new dawn turned to dusk
the setting sun
laid glorious to rest
across distant shores
of the mighty river
of Huckleberry fame
and alone I sit
'neath the afterglow
of bursting fiery hues
that so suddenly fade
and flow
as still the waters
so sweetly pass

Yet, hidden from view
a raging undercurrent
of memories
stirring once more
the unrest
of my soul
beset again
by darkness
and the stirring chirping
echo of the river's flow
Alone with only
the Shelby Forest air
and staring now deftly
into the tempest waves
my vision unfurled
and all becomes clear
those waters
that once as a child
I waded and played
and whose melodies
stirred the churning
of endless dreams
are the same waters
and veins that carried me here
this day
to sit along the shores
of Twain's magical River
where Huckleberry Finn
once stole free fare

Though the path
varied, may it be
the journey
be one and the same
what then would I be
and what might become of me
had I that day
allowed the Bluestone River
its sway and way with me
and adrift carried us
my raft and I
into the unknown fray

Yet, sweetly singing ever still
are the songs
of chirping endless
chirping
summertime frogs
the chorus and chords
still play
At long last
I have not yet
arrived
for endless be the sail
to the winds and waters
of my Huckleberry Dreams

DREAMS ADRIFT A CHRISTMAST GIFT

up on ridge
and upon places on high
beneath the dome
of a moonless sky
looking down
and peering downward way
the night adrift in a mist
a mysterious sway
and the mystical magic
of a jolly 'ol Nick
and his rustic red sleigh
that flies and soars
the world once around
yet only one night
this night, dare you make a sound

'tis early still
too early for him to appear
yet darkness captures the spell
of a dear child longing to hear
the clamor of bells
and the haughty
yet jolly laughter still
echoing above the clamoring crackle
of a near frozen chill
and the snow freely falling
slowly falling free
softly landing on branches
the endless weave of barren trees

the small frame house
an island nestled in a sea
a frozen blanket of white
purity
fields rolling to high rising ridges
a moment locked in an endless spree
of silence and calm
trapped in rapturous peace
captured within the subtle dance
of smoke rising
weaving a wavy stream
not given to chance

rather remnants of life
sustained by an ember glow
held within her walls
a fire burns
a potbellied stove
and the sweet serenade
a Victrola churns
the holiday sounds ring
softly Sinatra and Nat King Cole
"The Christmas Song" sings
to the chambers of time
and the creaking crackle
of near buckling walls
fending off an unforgiving foe
an unrelenting chill
and bitterly cold

yet to glance and peer
through six wood-framed panes
of glass frost stained
and strained
inside all is warm
with hearts and otherwise
though darkness prevails
cast and waiting for the spell
of the magical pine
cut and carried from a hillside
nearby
and neatly adorned
each decoration handmade
carefully crafted
and neatly ornate
not one the same

the darkness undaunted
a gentle flicker of embers
and the shimmer of lights
and hooks holding memories
ever cherished
trapped and held
within the reflection
glass balls of silver
and faded red

a four-room house
humble and hidden
so far removed
from the glamour and glitz

of big city lights
but not on this night
the night of all nights
for an only child
a sweet dreaming girl
her night and this moment
neither unrivaled nor unfurled
by any stream of metropolitan lights
anywhere in the world

and the only gift she will discover
beneath her glorious glitter filled
tree
will unleash all the joy
and magic
of a little girl's dreams
a brand-new doll
to love and to hold
to cradle and care
for the new life stitched
and sewn
by the magical weave
of mysterious bells

a daring journey
through fog and fray
dreams adrift, a Christmas gift
and the jolly old echo
of laughter
a man, his reindeer
and sleigh

FIRST DANCE AT LAST

her life she lived
by choice
humbly within the hills
and hollows
of the only place
she ever called home
a life lived long
and a long life
lived
upon the land she labored
and the home she made
laboriously
with such love

and though life at times
was not kind
in kind
she did respond with love
for eighty years
plus two
she lived each one
so well
and she lived them all
within the shadows
of such glorious hills
yet her light would rise
to unimaginable heights
by the love she shared
and the humble way

she cared
carried her spirit
around the globe
one-hundred-fold

chicken coups and pigs in pens
milk cows in the barn
each day then again
she cared for them
butter churned by churning
calloused hands and peeling
crisp sweet autumn apples
cooked in kettles
hovering over smoky
fire burning pits
brewing her brand and blend
of magic to pour
onto biscuits and bowls
filled to the brim
with a certain special
kind of love
found only in the rhythm
of a heartbeat and chorus
raised higher than the highest
of ridges and hills
of land she loved
and of the love
she bound
into every needle and stitch
of thread until a quilt
would cover us all

in the warmth
of sweet rising breads
she baked
pies and cobbler too
jams and jellies
fudge brownies cookies
and endless treats
she treated us all
a dozen times more
birthdays made special
and artistically sweet
whipped icing homemade
spread in delicate waves
beautifully bound
and brought with joy
wrought with love
like only she could
from her castle
a tiny country kitchen
safe and secure
behind the skeleton keyhole
door
dim lights flicker as winters
pass
passed once more
buried in banks of snow
could neither hinder her spirit
nor dampen the soul
of one so at peace
and peacefully so
she passed each day

like the first
pristine morning of spring
into the deep hold
of a cool mountain
summer night
free
falling into the strands
of an autumn's blend
of colorful chorus
yielding only to the chords
and bands of love
for life and those she so
loved
to gather and to give
a spoonful of mountain berry
jam
each one picked
by a thorn-pricked hand
when nary a snake
nor thickets of thorns
would impede her path
to the best berry patch
torn down the steep narrow way
without pause to cross
the crackling crystal brook
she would run-n-go
and land near the sweetest
golden apple patch
a harvest in hand
a bushel basket in tow
back home she strode

alone
yet never was she ever
really alone
for each bird that soared the sky
and every critter covered in fur
they were all known by her
and the winds and the gentle
rains
the crumble of leaves
and bite of bitter cold
she embraced them all
with a sweet serenade
and a humble smile
they in turn
held her safe
to yearn and to long
for one more day

she loved to learn
and forever longed to learn more
yet her father said
nine years of learning
was enough for a girl
but what is often said
is not all
and from those mountains
still
she would rise with unshakable will
and never will her strength
be denied
and never will I

nor any that ever
knew her love and grace
and that beautiful smiling face
forget the feeling
on the winds
beneath an angel's wings
as she breathes evermore

and that day
when her last day was near
and her last breath
would pass
but not until
we danced
barely could she rise
and no longer could she stand
alone
yet we needed to move
somewhere near
she needed to go from here
to just over there
but every move was a chore
how would we ever
reach the door
how would we manage
with one so proud
and full of grace
a failing body
left nary a trace
of the strength once bound
still she managed it all

as only she could
with a smile
and with grace
that could erase even time
as time stood still
her beaming face never failed
and lit every room
and touched our souls
until the very end

she had never lived
more than a mile
from where she was born
but no one I know
ever lived more
living further beyond
her life was so full
much fuller than most
and from such a tiny abode
her love circled the globe
she touched the lives
of all that she knew
she was the one
that no one dare dispute
she was beyond measure
she was beyond compare
yet in all of her years
never did I hear tell
never did she recall a story
of a time that she had
ever danced

so, in that moment
as the last sands
slowly sailed through the hour
of glass
into my arms she rose
and I asked
"may I have this dance"
with a lifetime of grace
slowly we strode
a mere shuffle of warm embrace
that first dance
was at last her chance
forever her smile
that shall never fade
and into forever
at last
she danced

SIMPLY

UNFURLS

and as you stand
standing there
so deeply ingrained
convicted by your own
convictions
unaware the shadows
of confliction
staring down, staring
down
staring down upon
your own reflection
images worn
shades of scorn
and blinders
forlorn
by the past
unable to pass
the belief of
believing all the truths
your doctrine held
true
yet betrayed
and still yet unaware
the truth betrays you
as what's true truly
unfurls
freely within the waves
of free thinking
winds
of change
and a dusting
of thoughts fleeting
and feathered
with each breath
anew

ONE-DIVIDE

what then
could one divide
if we were
but one
neither one to
conquer
nor conquerable
not paired
by our own
compare
one friend - one foe
no lines
drawn
no imaginary sand
no blood stained
swords
neither sticks nor
guns in hand
rather armed with
words
held in hands
open
to a mind
and a will
impassioned still
to listen and to
hear
words absent rue
for the winning

sees not an end
the race rules
the cost
and all becomes
lost
winning finds no
end
with merely
one-divide

RISE ABOVE

the winds of time
and echoes
of the waters
wail
from rivers winding
born of mountain streams
flowing freely onward
and distant shores
lakes so grand
and grandiose
north and south
more than mere words
and space
conjoined
our journey set sail
and a journeyman's tale
freely set free

stories told
of distant times
born anew
the minds
of young souls
yearning, yearning
to explore
the world of words
and still more
the world awaits
what's more than words

the swords of strength
courage and hope

take these reins
from my hand
take them as your own
journey on and onward
free
words in rhythm
neither pattern nor
rhyme
matters not in time
merely soar
a poet's spirit
set free
your journey
knows no bounds
fear not the fate
of a critic's hand
rise above all
that might tempt
your trying
for failure is found
only when silence
resounds
so use your words
be heard
rise above the noise
and victory
be yours

SIMPLY

TRUTH'S TOIL

the piercing sounds
of truth
the subtle sting
or voluminous blow
rather each or either
shall unbridle
the burdensome soul

perplexed by
one's own perspective
oft hidden well
within walls
of shimmering armor
and the afterglow
of self

Caste beneath shields
and buried still
deeper still
aligned majestically
the curse of perception
fueled and funneled
the course of fear

as dormant the truth
lain waiting
and the world awaits
invariably so it seems
yet all that which
will rise is
true
to be so bold
as to be
truly a friend
or rather still
one's darkest foe
from either end
undaunted and duly
free

set forth set free
upon the wisp
and whisper of wings
unfurled by the jaunt
of a journeyman's
quest

for verity be not
found
by mere want
of unfounded measure
rather measured by
the depths of longing
and toil

be that tragic
as it may...
to have lived
and laughed
and to know the depths
of fear
and the burning face
failure seared
and to have loved
even still

grander still
be the silent sounds
of power
freely set free
of dire and wanton
ghost
lurking still
in shadows unknown

THE CABIN

on ridge, on high
she stands
stately and yet
understated
her spirit soars
free
amidst wings of sprawling
rigid ridges
and barren trees
and the echo
of whispering pines

the waters below
ripple in endless random rows
of glisten and glow
in moonlit beams
and the waters that flow
from a river born
a million years or more
before
have etched their way
to grace her pass

yet, older still
than the waters
be the depths of her
soul

and by artful ax
mere centuries ago
were hand-hewn her walls
shaped unshapely square
ancient timbers bore ageless
logs
notched and stacked
in awkward flaws
though flawless
the air she breeds
and new life
she breathes
to each and all
so honored as to embrace
and grace her fold

warm as the love
of a swooning mother swan
she stands defiant
the cold
and tonight, all alone
most nights and days
her chambers filled
with only the solemn stillness
of dust lighting
on aged lumber
and creaking logs

the howling wind wails
above the clamoring chatter
a wet cluster of gathering mallards

and a bitter freeze
fills each crack, cranny
and crevasse
yet alone
never lonely is she
but rather filled
with the spirit and warmth
and the subtle power
of a single smile

for each day, beyond
the harrowing eastern hollow
a new day dawns
and embers that once
and always glow
from heart and hearth
linger still
as glorious the view
wayward the western shore
and with time
the colors may fade
and yield the day

and part ways we may
yet, never really
do we ever
depart

for the laughter of life
lingers
and the tears and embrace
of forever friends
like the wind
and her spirit
shall never end

simply

THE FARCE OF FEAR

what if we
were to lead
in every encounter
and each endeavor
and in every way
what if
empathy prevailed
and never swayed
from her seductive way
no, not merely
idealistic in fashion
and form
but rather passionate
in pursuit
of compassion
every thought, every action
and each intention
bound by peace
undaunted by the farce
of fear
what if we
were to listen first
and not merely lobby
to be heard
what if we were
to abandon the endless
senseless need to always
be right

the incessant need
to win
What if the power to prevail
prevailed first in thought
what if our arms race
raced to lend a hand
of help
and an ear yearning
to heal
what if we were
to imagine and live
only one race
the human race
what if empathy
prevailed
hand in hand
a land conquered
in peace
oh stop
stop your wretched fear
of evil's swell
for your fear
a fear so furiously
and fictionally
manufactured
is evil's fuel
for once stand tall
and lay down
your swagger and sword
lay them down
alongside your fear

for freedom's reign
is never found
wrapped in fear
but rather laced
in the pouring rain
of peaceful souls
stop this senseless
myriad of myth
of blood stained
waters of war
what if we were
to exhaust and expel
every ounce of every morsel
of our souls
in pursuit of peace
casting shadows upon
our undying need
to always be right
to win and
to conquer all
that simply disagree
what if it were
as simple as the swell
of rising sands
and empathy were
to always prevail

simply

IN FIELDS WE PLAY

in the stillness of night
and on the early morning
mountain ridges
and dark riverbanks
I shall miss you still
you became and would
become
so much of my soul
my being
together we shared
more than one life
could bear
together we trod
amidst darkness
and cold
together we became
and I shall miss you still
until once more
in fields we play
good night my friend
rest well

simply

THE WIND MY SOUL

the wind is howling, howling
the wind is growling
ripping through my skin
the wind is
howling
trees bending, bending
bending more
but will not break
but will
I
branches sway
in the howling
growling wind
angry waves dancing
angrily randomly
and somehow
majestic in sway
yet I stand
still
the wind is howling growling
ripping at my tattered
soul
standing in the dark fray
I'm smiling
still

59

OF AUTUMN

the rules
of autumn
as they may
rise with the
wind
each leaf bare
of barren trees
floating gently
aloft
with fluid grace
of a ballerina's
twirl
swirling freely
leaves falling free
bolden colors
bursting
from granular stems
scattered and strewn
from sticker bush
pins
of raspberry and holly
autumn's blend
spilled in spells
of rustic
hues
and grass never
greener
yet soon parched

and brown
covered in long
winding rows
and heaped in piles
random
colors defining
the rue
and rules
of autumn
shrouded in waves
a rolling sea
of mountains
and the endless
dome
of golden blue
and the whisper
of wind
my new, and only
friend
sweetly serenading
the secrets
of my soul
and of autumn

WATERFALLS

when
at last we sit
so near
the edge of time
and as time
we know
shall carry on
onward
toward the light
of a day
anew
but what's more
to explore
beyond the ledge
the falling waters
of a waterfall
run dry

and of time
no more
for ours
and the hours
when spent
with no more time
to tell
nary farce nor force
to face a final
farewell
what is lost

is only
time
for whatever time may
and whatever shall
be next
only time
may erase

MELODIOUS FRAY

to begin my day
amidst
the jumbled random
chorus of birds
is a day destined
divine

their melodies so sweet
and scattered strewn
or so it seems
to I
yet such tiny things
bound only
to be heard

the world they
own
this moment so
glorious
a moment to be
known
and freely sing
free

perched on high
they rest
in towering form
and sing
songs worth singing
with meanings
unknown
to I

a prelude
perhaps
to the winds
on which
they dance
rapid-fire burst
chirpity chirping
a melodious fray
of sweet
serenade

suddenly set sail
on air they float
and soar
their wings
own every breeze
and the sky
and the tops
of trees

assuredly
they soar free
and with each
dawn's new light
would they not
rather
do anything but
sing

simply

LITTLE ANGEL'S SMILE

the little angel's
smile
is warm
as the dawn's
first light
a concert of colors
breathing life
against your sky

you have slept
before
never viewing
in such light
yet a world
anew
awakes with you
as she rises
each day

what colors will
bring
what treasures to
find
what a joy
it must be
for you her guide
to be led this way

for is it you
bringing her
or is it she
bringing you

you open the doors
and she
brings you through
a venture so bright
so warm
so new
hold loose the reins
of this sojourn
you guide
guide only when
you must
for unknown the fate
and fate's sway
keep her safe
as you may
along the way

pause
with each frame
breathe
and capture
what you will
though the pendulum
is never
still

the rhythm will
vary
and flow
most oft
in staccato
dance in the colors
of the little angel's
smile
and your tears
of joy
a prism to form
an endless
rainbow

LONG TO AWAKEN

that place
one longs to escape
be the same
as that I long
to awaken
each day
as the one
before
and all those
to follow
absent eloquence
and decor
comfort is captured

the birth
of each day's dawn
seals the fate
the sun's slow
steady transgression
a stream
of enchantment
an evening sky
splashed with splendor
of light
departing
is no farewell
rather more
springs forth
an infinite well

rising once more
and more again
to quench
her endless glory

to dwell
in this place
in the wake
of timeless
swell
be not forsaken
rather still
polished metal
and medal
of honor
for her reward
be awarded
not merely of chance
rather more
that of a dream's
undying

ONE AMONG STALLIONS

I am but one
among the stallions
a herd
of wild and free
spirited stallions
we run as one
the herd

yet I am but one
among them
and we run
into the darkness
a moonlit night
a desolate land
known only to us
the herd

jaunting free
in a cloud dust
stampede
we run
because movement
is life
and freedom
the only sounds
I hear

the rapid fire
thumping
of bare galloping hooves
on barren land

the pounding rhythm
driving
my soul
a soul bound to run
but to whence
do we run
and to whence
do I
and now unaware
it is I
that presides the herd
a raging herd
of stallions
but to where
and where might they follow

suddenly aware
neither we lead
nor trail
but only we run
the moon fades
a sky so gray
and the pounding
rain
drowns clouds
of dust

calming my soul
a new pulsating
rhythm
nary slows the charge
of stallions

bolting blindly
into the night
into and through
groves of timber
and open
fields
the waters parting
in part
the path of galloping
hooves
the clapping of stones
thorns ripping
my flesh
spilling blood
onto the muddled
soil
of my soul

heavier the rain
numbs the pain
and white falling
flurries
the cold pardons
my discern
deep breathing

bursting lungs
one last breath
to stride on
onward we run
to live
living free

and what eludes
my reason to run
free
for freedom seldom lives
truly untamed
and as I live
as one
my soul to tame
in the midst
of the herd
a herd of stallions

simply

WINTER'S DUST

tiny flakes
float effortless
in the brisk
air
dancing in streams
of beauty
fields beneath ridges
a blanket of
calm
narrow paths
draped in snow
covered limbs
tunnel into unknown
depths
as seasons transform
my senses
keen to the woods
a world
open to its own
the wind for now
still
winter's dust
settles where it
may
I am invited
though I cannot
stay
still, she welcomes
me

no intrusion
an honored guest
I feel
for unaware
my admission already
earned
a crippling cold
so chill
would it not
preserve time
I gasp for more
this rare
breath of air
and yet to hold
such a gift
so rare
I long only
to repay
but what more
would add
to what has always
been
frozen still
by her endless
warmth
and received
into the fold
of folded arms
my only gift
of mere gratitude
exhaled

for therein
there is
no higher ground
than to barter equal
with the mother
of all

DREAMS

the gaze of my eyes
goes infinitely
inward

to a world my own
and places I long
to be

not a longing of
mere whim fantasy
but more

a place to escape
a new existence
create

images so real
feelings run so deep
swimming

in crystal blue waters
life warming my soul
and all

is at one with all
and into the sails
the wind

an effortless ride
now lost to my gaze
surreal

a world I create
dreaming dreams so real
unreal

more than mere image
much deeper the depths
in fact

dimensional views
with feeling and sound
astound

beyond notes dancing
the sounds you can touch
resound

I will ride this wave
the mist in my face
what's real

a mind unable
differentiate
endless

places longed for
inevitably
shall be

SHADOW OF ANGELS

in the shadows of angels
a spirit lingers
and that spirit
longs only
to dance
that spirit stirs restless
within us all
a spirit born
in our childhood days
that ran and played
free of care
unaware
that the world
might one day serve
as judge
serving judgement sometimes
cruel

but deep within
the spirit
we long only
to dance
to erase time
and the restraints
of self-consciousness
if only
for a moment
we could live
free

free enough
to allow our spirits
to soar
and to dance
and if that moment
could last for a moment
more
if only that moment
could last
forever

perchance that spirit
need only a breath
to awaken once more
imagine
if again
she danced

NO TRACKS IN THE SNOW

there are no tracks
in the snow
to lead
to this haven
of warmth
looking down
downward white waves
swirl and form
a whitecapped sea
to this island
of life

surrounded
so harsh
the surroundings
yet unthreatened
by threatening
extremes
she sustains
with such
grace
nearly eighty winters
have passed
most resting secure
within
this modest isle
an island of life

ridges so high
as to shadow
time
longing to engulf
as might
the angriest of seas
a deafening blanket
of chill
silently lands
and lays
upon her hand
enclosed her capsule
a haven defied
by time
yet this same brisk
and brittle air
so seemingly death
defiant
breathes life and yearns
for years
yet revealed

quite contrary
my initial glance
fades
this isle
of desolate days
yields the heart
of life
itself

for it is
from here
the arms called ridges
reach outward
reaching all realms
of the world beyond
a tower of encircling
walls
nipping at the rim
of clouds
as if to extend
and engulf
this tiny fortress
of warmth
but rather
nestled here
and cradled by
the sweetest scents
of oblivion

peering close
and closer still
crystal bars of ice
droop from the roof's
edges
their points buried
in drifts
of three feet of
drifting snow

from high above
peering down from
on high
what appears
a cage
with captives held
sealed in fate
yet the flicker
of an amber glow
glares a silent
angelic state
rather resting as fresh
as a newborn's
crib
she is longing
for nowhere
infinitely rejoiced
by the mere occasion
of simply being
here

from here
all the world
is at peace
for this piece
of land
entirely is her
world
though at times
she may
contemplate the conflicts

and wars
in places and lands
she has neither
nor ever will
see
but not this hour
and not this
night
the churn
and slow burn
below
of a burning furnace
is a source
but warmth's turn
here
is from the living
a place where most
would find themselves
lost
within the hour
which is surely
and sourly why
most end
in waging war

red birds and feathered
fowl
perched with the mourning
doves
express gratitude
unaware

a swinging cedar
hanging trove
filled
to the brim
she sustains them
and the barter
is fair
for filled within warm
aging walls
she smiles
through the panes
and pains
of time

the cat's bowl
refilled
though he may not
show face
until the face
of spring peers free
and yet
freely the dog
has abandoned her post
of running free
and nightly guard
of this isle's
sacred perimeter
just this side
of the fence
opting tonight instead
for the patch of rug

just this side
of the door
for any that might
and those that dare
lurk about
this desolate land
should not despair
she fears no
harm
and offers only
the welcome of love
and care

through the glimmer
of moonlit glow
two whitetail doe
trod
picturesquely unaware
beneath the pines
and snow capped
waters
of frozen ponds
an hour
and a moment
of such elegance
sustained
with such grace
warmly
she smiles
another quilt
another book

another hour of divine
contemplation
she is at home
indeed
longing for nowhere

SIMPLY

ABOUT THE AUTHOR

Joe Cundiff is a writer, novelist, and poet from Virginia. Living within the mountains of Appalachia and the enchanting weave of rivers therein, has provided the backdrop and inspiration for much of his writing. Joe is an avid outdoorsman, adventurer, and poet. Capturing the essence of all those experiences inspire him to write, and to share the depth of feeling held within each place. This is Joe's first collection of poetry.

You can find out more about Joe and his writing at the links below:

https://joecundiff.com/

https://YouTube.com/c/joecundiff

@joecundiffauthor

https://www.amazon.com/ (Joe Cundiff)

Made in the USA
Middletown, DE
14 December 2019